#It'saPandemic

Faced the Pandemic? This is for you

By Emmanuella Alausa

AuthorHouse™
1663 Liberty Drive
Bloomington, IN 47403
www.authorhouse.com
Phone: 1 (833) 262-8899

Because of the dynamic nature of the Internet, any web addresses or links contained in this book may have changed since publication and may no longer be valid. The views expressed in this work are solely those of the author and do not necessarily reflect the views of the publisher, and the publisher hereby disclaims any responsibility for them.

Any people depicted in stock imagery provided by Getty Images are models, and such images are being used for illustrative purposes only. Certain stock imagery © Getty Images.

Scripture quotations marked NIV are taken from the Holy Bible, New International Version®. NIV®. Copyright © 1973, 1978, 1984 by International Bible Society. Used by permission of Zondervan. All rights reserved. [Biblica]

This book is printed on acid-free paper.

ISBN: 978-1-7283-7904-3 (sc)
ISBN: 978-1-7283-7903-6 (e)

Print information available on the last page.

Published by AuthorHouse 10/01/2020

authorHOUSE®

Contents

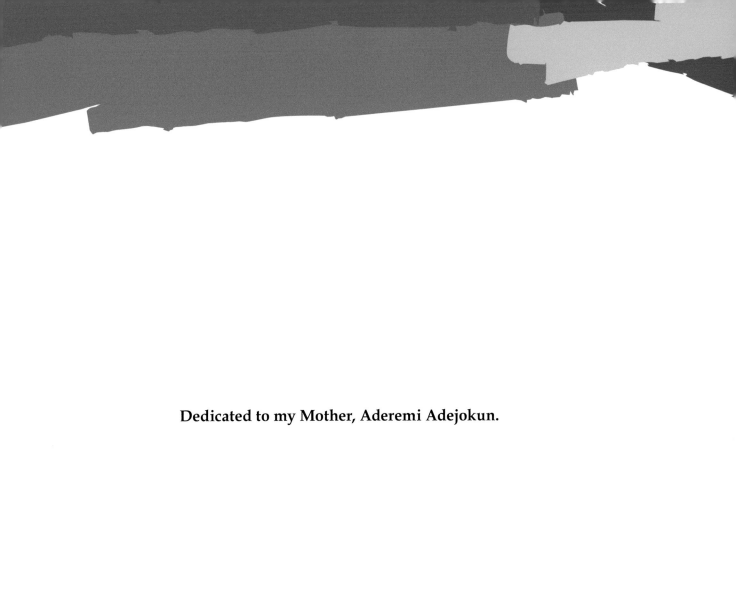

Dedicated to my Mother, Aderemi Adejokun.

No, in all these things we are more than conquerors through him who loved us. For I am convinced that neither death nor life, neither angels nor demons, neither the present nor the future, nor any powers, neither height nor depth, nor anything else in all creation, will be able to separate us from the love of God that is in Christ Jesus our Lord (Romans 8: 37-39).

Acknowledgement

Above all, I want to Thank GOD. Not an inch of this book would have been possible without the help of ALMIGHTY GOD and I am grateful. I feel so BLESSED.

I would also like to thank my family, especially my mum for encouraging me to write this book and for her constant motivation. Thank you. My late second Mum,Pastor Kate Ijeh, My amazing editor, Ms June Whittle, my 24/7 sister manager Marian Adejokun, Mr Oluseyi Obadare (Uncle Life Insurance) and the family, Mr Dapo, Pastor Caleb for his nurturing and reliable guidance, Pastors Clem and Marjorie Esomowei for their wisdom in teaching us how to pray effectively, Mrs Barbara & her son Peter Drake (our lovely neighbours)and The Falconer Family for all your love. I want to thank my drama teacher, Ms Lingham and all teachers.

The cover of #It'saPandemic is a book published by Emmanuella Alausa, a British children's & teenager's publisher, with illustrations by Onamusi Timilehin Folagbade, Chinyere Anosike and Kevin Le Moël.

Concerning the publication, there are two artists involved in the project. This was a chance to display their talents and a portrayal of inimitable gifts during the Covid-19 pandemic. These are youths we supported during this critical era. We ask you also to support them in their skills as we encourage other youths to thrive in their talent.

Please contact them via remiadejokun@yahoo.co.uk.

No, in all these things we are more than conquerors through him who loved us. For I am convinced that neither death nor life, neither angels nor demons, neither the present nor the future, nor any powers, neither height nor depth, nor anything else in all creation, will be able to separate us from the love of God that is in Christ Jesus our Lord (Romans 8: 37-39).

Breaking News

It's a pandemic! Living in London is a place I call home. A place full of adventure. From Buckingham Palace to the arcades, the fast food restaurants, to busy streets full of crowds brushing past each other concentrated on their journey. It's especially busy during the weekends or special times like Christmas, which is when you will see people gathering around in crowds. Cheering someone dancing or drawing in the centre. London is entertaining; it's all fun.

This is BBC news at ten. January 29th, with Sarah Richardson. "Here's our latest with the Breaking news: Today is the first day of a confirmed new virus case known as coronavirus here in the UK. We don't know the severity of this new virus which has surfaced. However, our hopes are that it doesn't spread, but we now understand that the person affected is being treated in hospital and is in a stable condition." Mehh! I did not think much about it. A virus all the way in Staycity Aparthotel, York and I'm in London, what are the odds? It did not occur to me then how fast a virus can spread and to be completely honest, I wasn't really concerned about it.

No, in all these things we are more than conquerors through him who loved us. For I am convinced that neither death nor life, neither angels nor demons, neither the present nor the future, nor any powers, neither height nor depth, nor anything else in all creation, will be able to separate us from the love of God that is in Christ Jesus our Lord (Romans 8: 37-39).

However, at the very far back of my head I was considering the potential outcome of school shutting down, and what that could mean to me or my friends and my Church.

"It's me Sarah Richardson again with the latest breaking news. Another 33 people have died due to the coronavirus also known as Covid-19 which raises the death toll to 104. Confirmed cases in the UK rose to 2,626 on Wednesday, from 1,950 on Tuesday. There have been 56,221 tests carried out in the UK for Covid-19, of which 53,595 were confirmed negative."

This is when I began to understand the severity of the virus and how other people's lives are drastically changing to this 'invisible killer'. The coronavirus is an infectious disease caused by a newly discovered coronavirus.

It spreads primarily through droplets of saliva or discharge from the nose when an infected person coughs or sneezes (World Health Organization, 2020), so this makes it hard to know when one has it. We are so used to people coughing or sneezing around us that we don't give it any attention. Well, now we do. Don't worry... GOD HAS US.

As the death tolls began to increase and more and more countries were suffering from the virus, schools, workplaces, clothing shops and anything that wasn't essential would be closed down. Leaving us all to quarantine in our homes, for however long we are meant to. #qauratineandchill.

After many days passing by, at times you can't help but feel to disregard the news and instructions given to us and just go out to live our best lives. Sometimes you just want to go to your friend's house or to the mall for a little retail therapy, as opposed to feeling enclosed with a jail like sense to it.

No, in all these things we are more than conquerors through him who loved us. For I am convinced that neither death nor life, neither angels nor demons, neither the present nor the future, nor any powers, neither height nor depth, nor anything else in all creation, will be able to separate us from the love of God that is in Christ Jesus our Lord (Romans 8: 37-39).

Although, you can exercise once a day and buy food, it just doesn't feel like….it doesn't feel normal. I miss the days I would take a little longer in the mornings to get my hair done because it was sunny outside, which equals pictures/videos on Snapchat, period pooh! Or, walking home from school with my friends and my sister slightly behind me tagging along. And going to the cinemas or planning an outing that I probably wasn't even going to go to. About now I would say 'good ole days' but I know we are going to get them back.

For example, in Victoria it is usually one of the busiest stations because it is where most people commute from home to work and vice versa. In this instance, during the pandemic, that was not the case.

No, in all these things we are more than conquerors through him who loved us. For I am convinced that neither death nor life, neither angels nor demons, neither the present nor the future, nor any powers, neither height nor depth, nor anything else in all creation, will be able to separate us from the love of God that is in Christ Jesus our Lord (Romans 8: 37-39).

Victoria Station Before the Pandemic

No, in all these things we are more than conquerors through him who loved us. For I am convinced that neither death nor life, neither angels nor demons, neither the present nor the future, nor any powers, neither height nor depth, nor anything else in all creation, will be able to separate us from the love of God that is in Christ Jesus our Lord (Romans 8: 37-39).

Victoria Station During the Pandemic

Image above illustrated by Timilehin Folagbade

No, in all these things we are more than conquerors through him who loved us. For I am convinced that neither death nor life, neither angels nor demons, neither the present nor the future, nor any powers, neither height nor depth, nor anything else in all creation, will be able to separate us from the love of God that is in Christ Jesus our Lord (Romans 8: 37-39).

Introduction

In the midst of what seemed like a whirlwind of anger, confusion and despair, my family and I strived to focus a good amount of our time on GOD. GOD to me is a friend that will always be with you even when you feel you're at your loneliest. He's our comforter when we feel weak and our solid rock that we lean on and stand on.

Praying was and is an essential part of our lives. We use our fears and worries and channel them into prayers. We would first thank GOD, for it says in the Bible, "In everything give thanks: for this is the will of God in Christ Jesus concerning you" (1 Thessalonians 5:18, King James Version). Then pray for the sick, people in authority, less privileged people, people who feel alone, people who feel suicidal, depressed, for protection and some many other prayer points. Staying at home also allowed us to build our relationship with GOD, so I guess there are a few benefits too.

Maybe this helped you to realise a few things too.

For some of us, staying indoors was like a reflection time which allowed us to we re-evaluate ourselves and ponder on our life. Maybe! What have we achieved? What is that special thing we are yet to do? What is our calling, that thing that fires up within you waiting to be busted out in life?

How can we accomplish our next innovation? What have we overcome? What do we want to do next? In as much as I felt a little helpless, I also felt motivated about things that I can do to help people. I found out that by using my social media platform I could do so many things for

No, in all these things we are more than conquerors through him who loved us. For I am convinced that neither death nor life, neither angels nor demons, neither the present nor the future, nor any powers, neither height nor depth, nor anything else in all creation, will be able to separate us from the love of God that is in Christ Jesus our Lord (Romans 8: 37-39).

the viewers to enjoy and learn. I would do a book review, discussing my highlights of the book I read and post it online.

I also enjoyed using my social media as a tool for spreading a few words of encouragement to share with young people. Even though I don't have tons of followers on my social media pages, I believe someone will be encouraged by my words on there and share my content with others.

Lockdown was stressful at times, because we have never experienced such a dramatic and sudden change to our daily routines. It felt like everything changed in the blink of an eye. I could tell some people found it hard to abide with rules in the early stages of the pandemic, by the pictures or videos they would post online. The news can bear witness to that. It made me perplexed as to why they cannot just stay at home for a while and let this thing pass over.

Hello people, my birthday is coming up. May the twelfth since you were wondering, yeah you. Having said that, some people were eager to release their full extrovert characteristics and have a little fun, to them that's all it seemed. It is understandable to some people that this was extremely difficult because they were so used to going out whenever they wanted, without any restrictions.

The thought of the virus killing thousands globally and shaking the earth so vastly, I'm sure, swings graciously above their heads but didn't perhaps enter it as much to stay at home. The saddest part is most of the time people don't even know they have it, therefore making it continue to spread and tragically killing people. It's heart-breaking.

No, in all these things we are more than conquerors through him who loved us. For I am convinced that neither death nor life, neither angels nor demons, neither the present nor the future, nor any powers, neither height nor depth, nor anything else in all creation, will be able to separate us from the love of God that is in Christ Jesus our Lord (Romans 8: 37-39).

In this book I will be describing key events that happened to me and my family during this pandemic.

As most of us probably did, I began to lose track of the days in the week. Some days felt like a Saturday even though it was Wednesday, or Tuesday felt like Thursday. In case anyone gets confused, I thought I should enlighten you that the initial days on the first line are what I presumed them to be. However, I was wrong. But the second line of dates are most likely right. Enjoy!

No, in all these things we are more than conquerors through him who loved us. For I am convinced that neither death nor life, neither angels nor demons, neither the present nor the future, nor any powers, neither height nor depth, nor anything else in all creation, will be able to separate us from the love of God that is in Christ Jesus our Lord (Romans 8: 37-39).

Vision of The Cure Covid-19

"A vision by God, illustrated by Aderemi Adejokun"

Maya Angelo -
When I Say I Am A Christian

When I say... 'I am a Christian' I'm not shouting 'I'm clean livin'' I'm whispering 'I was lost, Now I'm found and forgiven.'

When I say... 'I am a Christian' I don't speak of this with pride.
I'm confessing that I stumble and need Christ to be my guide.

When I say... 'I am a Christian' I'm not trying to be strong.
I'm professing that I'm weak and need His strength to carry on.

When I say... 'I am a Christian' I'm not bragging of success.
I'm admitting I have failed and need God to clean my mess.

When I say... 'I am a Christian' I'm not claiming to be perfect,
My flaws are far too visible but, God believes   I am worth it.

When I say... 'I am a Christian' I still feel the sting of pain..
I have my share of heartaches, so I call upon His name.

When I say... 'I am a Christian' I'm not holier than thou,
I'm just a simple sinner Who received God's good grace, somehow!

Jesus' death equals life for us all Hallelujah!

John 3:16
For God so lovedworld that he gaveone and only Son,whoever believeshim shall not perish but have eternal life.

Matthew 11:28
Come to me,you who are weary and burdened, and I will give you rest.

Matthew 28:20
...teachingto obey everything I have commanded you. And surely I am with you, to the very end of the age.

Jeremiah 29:11
For I know the planshave for you, declares the, "plans to prosperyou and not to harm you, plans to give you hope and a future."

2 Corinthians 5:17
Therefore, if anyone is in Christ,new creationcome.old has gone, the new is here!

1 Peter 5:7
Cast all your cares on him he cares for you.

Printed@ S&P 07830 018 495

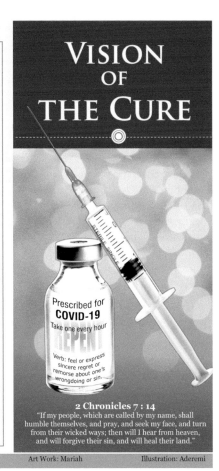

VISION OF THE CURE

Prescribed for
COVID-19
Take one every hour

REPENT

Verb: feel or express sincere regret or remorse about one's wrongdoing or sin.

2 Chronicles 7 : 14
"If my people, which are called by my name, shall humble themselves, and pray, and seek my face, and turn from their wicked ways; then will I hear from heaven, and will forgive their sin, and will heal their land."

Art Work: Mariah   Illustration: Aderemi

No, in all these things we are more than conquerors through him who loved us. For I am convinced that neither death nor life, neither angels nor demons, neither the present nor the future, nor any powers, neither height nor depth, nor anything else in all creation, will be able to separate us from the love of God that is in Christ Jesus our Lord (Romans 8: 37-39).

Hello my friends, I hope this tract finds you well as you read it , and its not to point a finger at anyone . I am a sinner saved by God's grace. Hallelujah.

As you know, the world is facing a pandemic crisis that has unfortunately claimed the lives of many, and still is . You may be confused, worried , upset or frustrated as to what is going on; more so because we can't do anything about it.

Can I reassure you my brothers and sisters that something good will come out of this . It shall pass over. Amen! It might be hard for you to accept this , but there is a God that loves and cares for us ,and knowns that this was going to happen .

This now brings me to the reason I am writing this message. I sat in my living room, not dreaming , not sleeping . I saw loads of people running helter-skelter, trying to que up for a vaccine and the individual (person) held a vaccine bottle with a black written message inside saying "Repent". The individual was going to inject the bottle; normally it is a liquid you get as a vaccine , but again what was in it was the word "Repent".

What does the word "Repent" mean? In the Webster dictionary , it says "to change one's mind, thus expressing regrets or sorrow for wrong doing . In the biblical sense of things , it says (Matthew 3:2) " Repent ye : for the kingdom of heaven is at hand" , and on Google it says , feel or express sincere regrets or remorse about one's wrong doing or sin".

The bible says "All have sinned and fallen short of the Glory of the God (Romans 3 :23). The vison that the Lord is showing us is the "cure" for all mankind which is in that bottle . "Repent" which ,means a complete change from BAD to GOOD . All I want my friends to know is to Repent, Believe and have Faith in God.

If you want to give your life to Jesus today , just say this prayer.

Salvation prayer : Surrendering your life to Christ .

1. Acknowledge in your heart that Jesus is Lord

2. Confess with your mouth that Jesus is Lord

3. Believe that Jesus died for your sins and was raised three days later for our justification.

4. Repent of your sins and get baptized in the name of Jesus Christ , and you shall receive the gift of the Holy Spirit to help you walk a new life in Christ .

Illustrated by Aderemi Adejokun
Artwork by Mariah Adejokun

No, in all these things we are more than conquerors through him who loved us. For I am convinced that neither death nor life, neither angels nor demons, neither the present nor the future, nor any powers, neither height nor depth, nor anything else in all creation, will be able to separate us from the love of God that is in Christ Jesus our Lord (Romans 8: 37-39).

Day 1
School's Out

I finished school earlier than other children in my school by two days, because of my mum who wanted to be cautious. At first, I was excited about leaving school earlier because there was no definite answer to when our school was shutting down even though other schools had shut down. There were just rumours spreading around that Friday would be our last day, but it wasn't for sure. I obviously told all my friends and took as many pictures and videos as we could. My sister and I weren't the first to precautiously leave school, by that time a bunch of students had left. I remember my Religious Education class looking more like a desert as opposed to our normal classes. My teacher, Mr O 'Donovan, was really nice. He would let us have more of a debate in our lessons while still learning the work we needed to. He certainly believed we were all able to achieve the highest grades possible. Surprisingly, Wednesday's class was a little more fun than usual. Even though he would say, "If school shutdown" or "If school happens to..." We all knew it was extremely close and that day I presume he did too. Unfortunately, there were those one or two teachers who liked to do their jobs to its maximum. Sometimes I wonder what our classes would be like if they took a day off.

No, in all these things we are more than conquerors through him who loved us. For I am convinced that neither death nor life, neither angels nor demons, neither the present nor the future, nor any powers, neither height nor depth, nor anything else in all creation, will be able to separate us from the love of God that is in Christ Jesus our Lord (Romans 8: 37-39).

Teachers were and still are an essential part of my life. They help us grow into people we are today and equip us with knowledge to blossom into adults of excellence.

A couple particular teachers I appreciate are Mr Todd and Ms Ramdeen. Mr Todd works so hard, coming into school at six or seven volunteering his time to help children who needed extra help. Sometimes I wondered, does he sleep.... he always gave words of encouragement. Ms Ramdeen is a bit strict but still shows her kind heart and fun side in our lessons. Thank you.

No, in all these things we are more than conquerors through him who loved us. For I am convinced that neither death nor life, neither angels nor demons, neither the present nor the future, nor any powers, neither height nor depth, nor anything else in all creation, will be able to separate us from the love of God that is in Christ Jesus our Lord (Romans 8: 37-39).

PEWW, PEWW, PEWW. The school tannoy (they are a British manufacturer of loudspeakers and public-address systems) rang at 3:15pm as expected. My head teacher gave her typical speech, to stay clear from the roads, always be safe and of recently added for us to continuously wash our hands. I left my last class of that day, not quite knowing what the future holds, and went home.

School during the pandemic

No, in all these things we are more than conquerors through him who loved us. For I am convinced that neither death nor life, neither angels nor demons, neither the present nor the future, nor any powers, neither height nor depth, nor anything else in all creation, will be able to separate us from the love of God that is in Christ Jesus our Lord (Romans 8: 37-39).

This is our school hall. Empty assembly halls, with no students to listen to the Headteacher's speech.

No, in all these things we are more than conquerors through him who loved us. For I am convinced that neither death nor life, neither angels nor demons, neither the present nor the future, nor any powers, neither height nor depth, nor anything else in all creation, will be able to separate us from the love of God that is in Christ Jesus our Lord (Romans 8: 37-39).

Day 2
We @ home

It's now a Thursday and I am living my first day at home as a home-schooled student. Prior to us leaving, my teachers had given us a hefty folder with every subject each individual student studied, to do over the next weeks. So I was good for a while plus we had online work too. It makes me wonder how home-schooled children feel about quarantine. I went to a public secondary school and to be honest, I wouldn't trade it for a prestigious school. There are some memories that are truly irreplaceable and friendships that I am Blessed to be in. I have always been an outgoing and chatty person and the detentions most certainly testify to that, so I never found it hard to speak to new people. In as much as I didn't find making friends hard, I knew some people did so as I got older, I wanted to make them feel more included and not spoken to anyway because of their character. I hope I made at least one person feel loved. While I was at home, most of my friends were at school. So, in our Health and Social Care lessons they FaceTimed me to show me what they were doing. How sweet! Our teacher, Ms Henry, has always been nice to us.

Apart from the very much appreciated FaceTime call, I was mostly on my phone, repeatedly eating, watching movies, and thinking of all the new episodes I can watch. Oh, my days. I love Real Housewives of Atlanta and Greenleaf. Yesssss! This year is the last season of Greenleaf and Ms Oprah I am sad about that, literally an amazing show.

No, in all these things we are more than conquerors through him who loved us. For I am convinced that neither death nor life, neither angels nor demons, neither the present nor the future, nor any powers, neither height nor depth, nor anything else in all creation, will be able to separate us from the love of God that is in Christ Jesus our Lord (Romans 8: 37-39).

Day 3
Fun Day Friyay

Fun day Friday friyay! It was Friday as you probably guessed, and I woke up later than usual. Me and my sister helped my mum get ready for work by doing her hair, makeup and picking out a cute outfit. My mum works as a teacher assistant in a special needs school and she absolutely loves it. She says it is very rewarding and the children love her friendly and bubbly personality. Sometimes she would even shed tears talking about them. She misses them a lot. Since we are talking about my mum then I should tell you how strong, ambitious, outgoing, loud and funny she is. She is a whirlwind of laughter, but she doesn't let that fool you ... she is strict too. To GOD be the Glory. She has four beautiful girls, if I do say so myself, and an energetic dog.

Once my mum left for work, which was one of her temporary last days, me and my other sister would eat anything and everything, most likely pancakes. Our schedule went a bit like this; on our phones, eat again then cleaned a bit. Then my mum would be home, following my other sister from work.

No, in all these things we are more than conquerors through him who loved us. For I am convinced that neither death nor life, neither angels nor demons, neither the present nor the future, nor any powers, neither height nor depth, nor anything else in all creation, will be able to separate us from the love of God that is in Christ Jesus our Lord (Romans 8: 37-39).

Day 4
Adapting

It is Saturday now and we probably woke up around 11:00am. Maybe it was just me, because I can sleep a lot. After eating we brought a few things to eat and then snack on as well and a lot of dog food. We would watch movies as a family. That soon became our new hobby and sometimes we ate popcorn or cheesy nachos while watching the movie.

No, in all these things we are more than conquerors through him who loved us. For I am convinced that neither death nor life, neither angels nor demons, neither the present nor the future, nor any powers, neither height nor depth, nor anything else in all creation, will be able to separate us from the love of God that is in Christ Jesus our Lord (Romans 8: 37-39).

Day 5

Bored In

I woke up and ate. Then I watched movies and slept late.

No, in all these things we are more than conquerors through him who loved us. For I am convinced that neither death nor life, neither angels nor demons, neither the present nor the future, nor any powers, neither height nor depth, nor anything else in all creation, will be able to separate us from the love of God that is in Christ Jesus our Lord (Romans 8: 37-39).

Day 6
The House

I woke up late, had breakfast, of course I ate. Had loads of snacks. We watched a few movies and hit the sack.

No, in all these things we are more than conquerors through him who loved us. For I am convinced that neither death nor life, neither angels nor demons, neither the present nor the future, nor any powers, neither height nor depth, nor anything else in all creation, will be able to separate us from the love of God that is in Christ Jesus our Lord (Romans 8: 37-39).

Day 7

I woke up late…again. At this point I pushed myself to look at some of my work that I needed to do. I aimed to try and put a lot of effort in my schoolwork so that if I were to have a test, I would be able to do well.

I aimed to do at least three hours of work every day, which thinking about it, isn't a lot at all. In all honesty, some days I didn't feel like working at all, maybe because I was stuck at home doing the same thing every day.

No, in all these things we are more than conquerors through him who loved us. For I am convinced that neither death nor life, neither angels nor demons, neither the present nor the future, nor any powers, neither height nor depth, nor anything else in all creation, will be able to separate us from the love of God that is in Christ Jesus our Lord (Romans 8: 37-39).

Day 10 -15
New York, New York

The deaths continued to spark high. The results continuously fluttered just like peoples' fear and confusion of the virus. The death tolls were shocking, and the positive cases recorded were absolutely astonishing, over millions of cases all over the world. I couldn't even begin to comprehend the unrecorded cases. It was so sad. May their families find comfort. The people in New York were particularly affected at one point.

New York was becoming the epicentre of coronavirus deaths. From each day it seemed every six hours bad news would reoccur about the deaths in New York. Even though I have never been to New York, I always saw it as a place of beauty.

After watching 'Home Alone: Lost in New York', I felt a strong connection for New York and knew that one day I will go there (preferably at Christmas). New York reminded me of fun, laughter and adventure. I especially wanted those chocolate chip cookies from the movie 'Home Alone'. They looked so soft.

However, as a result of the pandemic it was not illustrated that way. As mentioned on Bloomberg news, almost all indicators showed that the Covid-19 outbreak in New York was still the worst in the U.S.

The BBC stated that the 731 fatalities reported brought the total to 5,489 deaths and 138,836 infections. People in the U.S. black community were distinctly infected by the virus.

No, in all these things we are more than conquerors through him who loved us. For I am convinced that neither death nor life, neither angels nor demons, neither the present nor the future, nor any powers, neither height nor depth, nor anything else in all creation, will be able to separate us from the love of God that is in Christ Jesus our Lord (Romans 8: 37-39).

This could have been because of underlying issues or the fact that a majority of black people deal with obesity, high blood pressure and diabetes. GOD IS IN CONTROL.

No, in all these things we are more than conquerors through him who loved us. For I am convinced that neither death nor life, neither angels nor demons, neither the present nor the future, nor any powers, neither height nor depth, nor anything else in all creation, will be able to separate us from the love of God that is in Christ Jesus our Lord (Romans 8: 37-39).

New York! New York! Poem

New York ! New York ! A city that hits you with lights.

A city mentioned twice.

It's up to you New York,

Take on this fight

To choose to battle this thing

And not give up.

Pretend like it is a dream,

Or think it is bad luck.

The virus prowled on anyone and what felt like everyone.

It gave no warning...

It hit like a gun.

Children stayed at home, saying "Mummy it's boring"

Just to wake up to the same routine the next morning.

What can we do in times like this except pray and be thankful?

To GOD, the nurses, doctors and everyone who helped,

The big and the small,

We appreciate it all.

What made you angry?

Was it the empty shelf?

Parents crying out for help,

Not knowing the last minutes of how loved ones felt.

Hearing that people died

But not really sure why,

No, in all these things we are more than conquerors through him who loved us. For I am convinced that neither death nor life, neither angels nor demons, neither the present nor the future, nor any powers, neither height nor depth, nor anything else in all creation, will be able to separate us from the love of God that is in Christ Jesus our Lord (Romans 8: 37-39).

This invisible killer, could it fly?
It travelled so fast,
Anyone could get it in a blink of an eye.
GOD IS our refugee
And that's why.
I choose GOD for my life.
New York City you can beat this!

New York City

No, in all these things we are more than conquerors through him who loved us. For I am convinced that neither death nor life, neither angels nor demons, neither the present nor the future, nor any powers, neither height nor depth, nor anything else in all creation, will be able to separate us from the love of God that is in Christ Jesus our Lord (Romans 8: 37-39).

Day 8

To me it felt like the days were basically repeating itself after a while. Luckily, we would do something fun making me forget why we can't just go outside. Then I remembered that there's a virus, duhh. To keep ourselves occupied we would constantly bake until there's no flour or eggs left in the house. Sometimes it was a sibling's competition even though we would show support to each other, we wanted to see who was better at baking. My sister made a cookie dough kind of cake that tasted sooo good and I attempted to make a replica. However, mine had more salt than required, leaving my tongue with a tangy taste to it. My sister on the other hand, made lemon drizzle cake for the first time and it turned out good. It was actually fantastic. In all honesty when I bake, I like to look at a recipe once or twice then just go with the flow and use any alternatives, if I don't have the suggested ingredients. My sister likes to follow the recipes to the T and rarely adapts the recipe unless she wants to add her own uniqueness. I can still kind of bake though. I got skills, don't worry.

No, in all these things we are more than conquerors through him who loved us. For I am convinced that neither death nor life, neither angels nor demons, neither the present nor the future, nor any powers, neither height nor depth, nor anything else in all creation, will be able to separate us from the love of God that is in Christ Jesus our Lord (Romans 8: 37-39).

Day 13
Most Likely Day 20-ish Chilled

The next few days were basically the same. I would go to bed very late then wake up late too, watch shows/movies and so on. The latest I went to bed was around 7:00am. I'm a night person. I actually began to lose track of how many days we had been indoors. To me it didn't seem that long. The first week or two were a bit mehh, but that was probably because my sister was still at work and so was my mum, plus my uncle wasn't here yet. Eventually my sister began working from home and my mum temporarily stopped working. Despite everything, ALMIGHTY GOD still provided for us and HE still does. I really give GOD Allll the Praise and Adoration because sometimes I truly wonder how life would be without the presence of GOD in our life. THANK YOU, JESUS.

My sister and I were still tackling this thing called baking. Erstwhile, my sister had finally started her business in cooking after finding her passion for cooking and baking; c_cuisine, (follow her on Instagram) and was getting a few orders too. She definitely progressed as quarantine continued. While at home she made a range of cakes - marble, chocolate, sprinkle, coconut, lemon drizzle, banana, red velvet, different cupcakes and soon to make my birthday cake. #excited

All our bakes were good, apart from the time my other sister hastily decided to join the baking team and did an appalling bread like 'cake' with mountains of icing spread all over the top then shamefully topped with sprinkles. How can she use half a box of a big icing sugar on such a small cake? Thank GOD she's intelligent and ambitious. Be that as it may, she did do amazing sprinkle cupcakes, probably the best I've ever had. I would like to personally thank Tesco for the ready-made cupcake mix, delicious.

No, in all these things we are more than conquerors through him who loved us. For I am convinced that neither death nor life, neither angels nor demons, neither the present nor the future, nor any powers, neither height nor depth, nor anything else in all creation, will be able to separate us from the love of God that is in Christ Jesus our Lord (Romans 8: 37-39).

Day 25 or Something

(I only chose it because it is in-between 20-30)

Before the global lockdown, my family and I would minister at Churches, events and other places to put a smile on people's faces and spread GOD'S love. Our ministering name is called The Levites. To keep up with our performing we did an online dance where we took videos of us dancing and posted it online to encourage and motivate people to stay calm and peaceful during this hard time. We can overcome this, by The Blood of Lamb and the Word of our Testimony. At this moment, we have done about five or six dances in total, which resulted in lots of people feeling blessed and inspired by it. Even well-known artists or people who wrote the song we danced to replied to our ministering.

No, in all these things we are more than conquerors through him who loved us. For I am convinced that neither death nor life, neither angels nor demons, neither the present nor the future, nor any powers, neither height nor depth, nor anything else in all creation, will be able to separate us from the love of God that is in Christ Jesus our Lord (Romans 8: 37-39).

My family and I dancing Praise & Worship during Lockdown
Visit The Levites Worship Website on www.thelevitesworship.com

No, in all these things we are more than conquerors through him who loved us. For I am convinced that neither death nor life, neither angels nor demons, neither the present nor the future, nor any powers, neither height nor depth, nor anything else in all creation, will be able to separate us from the love of God that is in Christ Jesus our Lord (Romans 8: 37-39).

Today it is Probably Day 20

No, it's Actually Day 30

It's amazingly scary how we are all living in such a surreal moment that will most likely be taught in classes in the years to come, and celebrated by people who helped during this time to keep us all safe. We are living in history. In as much as some people are doing okay in this time, there are people everywhere, as well, who aren't adjusting to their new 'norm'.

For example, in Nigeria, a county I am proud to say I am from despite its many inconsiderate flaws, there are a lot of people struggling to make ends meet.

My mum has a charity called Relief Africa, a Non-Profit Charity Organisation, which she has founded for over 10 years now. Relief Africa supports and empowers children and families who are economically and socially disadvantaged across the UK, Nigeria, Ghana, etc. My mum frequently get calls on WhatsApp from people asking for help and explaining the struggles they are going through, and it isn't being mentioned on the news nor are they being assisted. As she is only one woman with a family of her own, it can be hard to help everyone that you would wish to. In Nigeria, unless you're born with a silver spoon in your mouth, then you have to work extremely hard to be in a comfortable position.

No, in all these things we are more than conquerors through him who loved us. For I am convinced that neither death nor life, neither angels nor demons, neither the present nor the future, nor any powers, neither height nor depth, nor anything else in all creation, will be able to separate us from the love of God that is in Christ Jesus our Lord (Romans 8: 37-39).

Day 35 or so
Seal-ling Not Sealed

I woke up that morning feeling blessed and thankful for GOD waking my family and I up. I did my exercise, because like most people I was one of them who didn't want to look the same after quarantine. But I don't know how that is meant to work when all we can do is eat and snack, and eat and snack, and eat. Most of us want to look snatched but there's always something we don't necessarily like about ourselves. However, we should embrace it if it is something we cannot change and accept how GOD made us. I did my healthy food cooking that day and watched a few shows. Then my sister said she wanted to do another exercise that night to compensate for any bad habits during the day. Suddenly, we heard a banging sound almost coming from the ceiling.

We both heard it. A few seconds later we looked at each other, paced to the hallway and then heard my sister say, "Mum, the ceiling is falling in our room". What? Why? How? Why does the ceiling have to fall now during this pandemic? Why does it have to fall at all? Who will fix it during this time and how much will it cost? I was in shock to what was happening because there was no sign previously of damage to the ceiling in our room, so it was a surprise. A rather unpleasant surprise. As we ran upstairs, we saw the ceiling lowering with water pressuring it down.

In the spur of the moment we started to pack all the essential things we needed, so that we could evacuate as quickly as possible.

As my mum was making urgent phone calls, my sister and uncle were trying to move things to prevent a massive damage or to avoid things getting wet. Just as they were moving things… Pewssshhh!!!

No, in all these things we are more than conquerors through him who loved us. For I am convinced that neither death nor life, neither angels nor demons, neither the present nor the future, nor any powers, neither height nor depth, nor anything else in all creation, will be able to separate us from the love of God that is in Christ Jesus our Lord (Romans 8: 37-39).

"Get downstairs! Get downstairs all of you, now."

The ceiling had drastically fallen. Then to make matters worse my mum was suffering from a high temperature and feeling really tired. She had lost her appetite and sometimes felt cold then hot, all the symptoms of Covid-19. Thank GOD it was not Covid. Prayers really do work.

The water had gushed out as they were moving things around, so they rapidly left the room, and my heart stopped for like two seconds in fear. The sound was so scary. In my mind I'm like okay so we have two options.

1. Go to my sister's house. I didn't mind although it was a bit small for all six of us but perfect for two people. Plus, she doesn't have all the good food like our house does; sometimes it can be a bit boring.

2. The second option was to go to a hotel. Now when I am thinking of a hotel, I think luxurious and comfy, so comfy that I don't want to leave. If we were going to go to a hotel it would have to be in West End because that is where the nice ones are located. Who doesn't like to feel boujee!

Hold up... wait a minute. I wanted to do this, but to go to these places we would need transport because my mum didn't have a car. What to do now? Despite the sudden scare we eventually had to come to a conclusion to stay in the house. We called the people who fix damages in houses and still stayed in the house.

THANK GOD!

No, in all these things we are more than conquerors through him who loved us. For I am convinced that neither death nor life, neither angels nor demons, neither the present nor the future, nor any powers, neither height nor depth, nor anything else in all creation, will be able to separate us from the love of God that is in Christ Jesus our Lord (Romans 8: 37-39).

No, in all these things we are more than conquerors through him who loved us. For I am convinced that neither death nor life, neither angels nor demons, neither the present nor the future, nor any powers, neither height nor depth, nor anything else in all creation, will be able to separate us from the love of God that is in Christ Jesus our Lord (Romans 8: 37-39).

Day 28 Maybe, Not Too Sure I Made it up
I Found Out it is Surprisingly Day 40

Compelled to stay at home magnified me to things I could be doing and what I want to be doing. I discovered my love for reading. It's just so fun, and it takes you to another realm and allows you to be in your zone. I always thought that I knew what I wanted to be when I'm older, maybe a teacher or actress but I decided no. I want to have more than one profession and possibly more than one degree. I want to be so many things by the Grace of GOD. Perhaps a fashion designer, and a teacher, and a motivational speaker, and lawyer, and an actress to infinity and beyond.

The sky is just the beginning. I was on Instagram one night and happened to find myself on Oprah Winfrey's page. After viewing a few videos and photos, I found the one with Michelle Obama. For real, the day I meet these two world changing women I…I might cry. A……. Anyways, sorry I was wiping my tears imaging the day. Mrs Michelle Obama was wearing a blue jumpsuit with a few other colours by the side and had a volumed beautiful curly hairstyle. When she said something along the lines of "I dislike when children are asked what they want to be when they grow up….they can be so many things." I was completely astounded when I heard that, not only because it was the first time I had heard that, but also because we shared the same views. It made me smile inside. "I can do all things through CHRIST who strengthens me" (Philippians 4:13).

We can do anything we put our minds and efforts into. What you put in is what you get out and sometimes even more good is produced because of the favour from GOD.

No, in all these things we are more than conquerors through him who loved us. For I am convinced that neither death nor life, neither angels nor demons, neither the present nor the future, nor any powers, neither height nor depth, nor anything else in all creation, will be able to separate us from the love of God that is in Christ Jesus our Lord (Romans 8: 37-39).

It inspired me to explore new things and start an adventure on my career.

During this time, I think it is important that we try to hear from GOD and listen to what GOD has to say to us. Some people find that in the centre of trauma and sadness is the best times that they can find peace and speak to GOD. One of the things I enjoy doing to grow in my relationship with GOD is listening to Joyce Meyer. She has a message called 'Hearing From GOD'. She has a lot of wise words to say and how to lives a righteous life. So far, I enjoy listening to her because she has similar stories like me; they relate to everyday life and she is a role model. When we are on our walk/journey with GOD I think it is important to not fear.

The acronym for fear is fake evidence appearing real and we have to pray against it so that peace and love and faith can replace it. As it says in 2 Timothy 1:7, "For God hath not given us the spirit of fear; but of power, and of love, and of a sound mind."

So, let's pursue to live a life full of freedom with GOD and enjoy our life. After listening to TD. Jakes, another preacher I enjoy listening to, I started to feel encouraged by his message. He said begin to plan your victory. His main scripture was Mark 10:30. "But he shall receive an hundredfold now in this time, houses, and brethren, and sisters, and mothers, and children, and lands, with persecutions; and in the world to come eternal life."

This basically says that we will be blessed on this earth but with persecution (harsh words and fake friends for example) but we can strive through it because GOD is greater than it all. AMENNN!

No, in all these things we are more than conquerors through him who loved us. For I am convinced that neither death nor life, neither angels nor demons, neither the present nor the future, nor any powers, neither height nor depth, nor anything else in all creation, will be able to separate us from the love of God that is in Christ Jesus our Lord (Romans 8: 37-39).

Day 51...mehh
At Least I Know it is May 12th

12ᵗʰ, I am so excited...it's my sixteenth birthday yayyy. ALLL THE PRAISE TO GOD MOST HIGH. I have literally been planning how my sixteenth birthday would look like, for sixteen years, maybe. For some reasons, I feel like being sixteen is literally one of the most, if not the most, important milestone of one's life. It just feels so special. That day, my neighbour's children had spent the night and my two older sisters were there too.

In the morning we woke up and prayed. It is very important that we give GOD thanks. Not just for the little things, but always. For example, waking up, being able to move some part of our body, being able to breathe and so much more. We did some exercises, P.E with Joe. You would think it would be much simpler as it is mainly for kids, but no, we all felt the burn. Collectively, after exercise we started decorating and getting ready. The decorations were elegant but simple. It was a mixture of white, gold and silver balloons dangling from the sealing and fairly secured by sellotape. The dining table had a plain white sheet that was covered with party poppers, tiaras, drinks, cups, fruit punch dispenser and napkins. To elaborate the table we graced the other things on the table with BBQ ribs, BBQ chicken wings, BBQ drumsticks, hot dogs, chicken and bacon filled sandwiches, fried potatoes, cornbread, corndog, corn on the cob and big prawns. Normally, I would have a big gathering or celebrate my birthday especially as it is my sixteenth, but this year was different. Instead my mum came up with the marvellous idea to do a virtual party.

No, in all these things we are more than conquerors through him who loved us. For I am convinced that neither death nor life, neither angels nor demons, neither the present nor the future, nor any powers, neither height nor depth, nor anything else in all creation, will be able to separate us from the love of God that is in Christ Jesus our Lord (Romans 8: 37-39).

Birthday Glow

The party would take place on an app called Zoom where up to 100 plus people can join. Lots of family and friends tuned in around 3pm. We had our neighbour playing happy birthday on the piano, my mum doing a comedy entrance, all of us dancing to music and then the cutting of the cake. It was so busy but full of laughter. I really enjoyed myself that day. I was thankful.

We actually had two cakes. One chocolate cake from Costco and one my sister made, kind of.... some cake boxes may or may not have helped. We had them with some ice cream.

On my birthday my friends had the option to come and get contact free food and of some them did which was nice. Shout out to Dani. Believe it or not, by 6:30pm I was sleeping, for like 30-45 mins, then I woke up and remembered that it was my birthday and I can sleep tomorrow, all day tomorrow. I ate corn dog and some more cake and some more ice cream and some more chicken and some more prawns. Then we all watched a movie at night time.

THANK YOU, JESUS for a great Birthday!

No, in all these things we are more than conquerors through him who loved us. For I am convinced that neither death nor life, neither angels nor demons, neither the present nor the future, nor any powers, neither height nor depth, nor anything else in all creation, will be able to separate us from the love of God that is in Christ Jesus our Lord (Romans 8: 37-39).

No, in all these things we are more than conquerors through him who loved us. For I am convinced that neither death nor life, neither angels nor demons, neither the present nor the future, nor any powers, neither height nor depth, nor anything else in all creation, will be able to separate us from the love of God that is in Christ Jesus our Lord (Romans 8: 37-39).

Day, the Day Before my Birthday

Let me take you back a couple of hours to make it clear why our neighbour's children were at our house despite social distancing. I know some of you were thinking my actions were illegal. As you know, my birthday was the next day so my mum, uncle and I went to Costco to get some food. While we were travelling to Costco my mum received a call from my sister saying how our neighbour wanted my sister to go to their house and pray for his wife. My mum didn't quite understand what she was saying because her phone is so old fashioned. She asked plenty of questions like did you wear your mask and gloves and wrap your face and wear loads of clothes before stepping out the house, and take off all your clothes before re-entering our house? My mum could not understand clearly what my sister was saying so then they agreed to resume the conversation later. About two minutes afterwards, she started getting agitated to why she went. I suspect she remembered that there is a virus going around, and wondering why did she not just pray for them in our home? I understood why my mum was angry because we did not know what was wrong with our neighbour and it did not help that we could not apprehend all that was being said. She sighed and said, "let's pray".

We sang a song and prayed under our breaths for a while. Yes, on a bus.

No, in all these things we are more than conquerors through him who loved us. For I am convinced that neither death nor life, neither angels nor demons, neither the present nor the future, nor any powers, neither height nor depth, nor anything else in all creation, will be able to separate us from the love of God that is in Christ Jesus our Lord (Romans 8: 37-39).

Image illustrated by Chinyere Anosike

After getting all our delicious goodies at Costco we arrived at home and my sister finally told us what had happened. Even though my sister had explained everything it was only when she was explaining again and pointed to our neighbour's house across the road that my mum knew which neighbour it was.

Initially, we thought it was our neighbour who is an old lady and that was another reason to get worried, because elderly people were the group of many who sadly were affected by the virus

No, in all these things we are more than conquerors through him who loved us. For I am convinced that neither death nor life, neither angels nor demons, neither the present nor the future, nor any powers, neither height nor depth, nor anything else in all creation, will be able to separate us from the love of God that is in Christ Jesus our Lord (Romans 8: 37-39).

more. In the clarity of it all, my mum rushed out of her seat, dropped her plate on the table and paced to their house.

4:30pm – Knock! Knock! Knock! Knock! No one answered. 4:32pm - Knock! Knock! Knock! Knock! No one answered. 4:35pm- Knock! Knock! Knock! Knock! No one answered.

My mum began to be disquiet, so we continued prayer.

4:45 Knock! Knock! Knock! Knock! No one answered.

This time it was a different response but not from whom we wanted. Their neighbour opened the door, acknowledging our repeated knocking, saying that he does not know where they went but our neighbour's wife was apparently acting strange the night before.

The neighbour said that the wife had gone into the garden the night before, with a Bible and no shoes, and gave her neighbour her engagement ring. That was such a strange thing to do. With the information we had we could not do anything but pray and hope for the best.

A few hours later, our neighbour who we were worried about, said that his wife was with her sister and that it was the battle of the mind that was affecting her. I didn't quite get it until it was later described to me as something similar to mental health issues. We continued praying for her and her family while also checking on our neighbour. At around 11:00pm after praying, my mum and uncle decided to check on them again. After coming back, we prayed for a few minutes and then I saw her putting on her shoes, her jumper and her jacket.

I asked, "Where are you going? Are you going to pick up his wife from his sister's house?"

No, in all these things we are more than conquerors through him who loved us. For I am convinced that neither death nor life, neither angels nor demons, neither the present nor the future, nor any powers, neither height nor depth, nor anything else in all creation, will be able to separate us from the love of God that is in Christ Jesus our Lord (Romans 8: 37-39).

She courageously responded, "Just in case." She wasn't even certain herself.

My mum is a very strong and determined woman who always puts other people's needs before hers, so need not to say I was not surprised. Our neighbour and my family came to a conclusion that it was necessary to go to pick up his wife, which was all the way in Slough. That was very far, especially when you take the wrong exit on the motorway, as they did.

My sisters and I had the duties and responsibility of taking care of our neighbour's children. They are so adorable and polite. That night we prayed for their mum, made hot chocolate with sprinkled pancakes, watched a movie, played the game called Uno, played twenty one dares even though one is nine and one is four and then we went to sleep. Oh yeah, how could I forget, they were compelled to sing happy birthday to me! I REALLY THANK GOD FOR LIFE.

Two years ago, IN December, I was hit by a car and I went through the worst pain ever. I still remember coming back from the hospital with a massive foot. Unfortunately, it was raining that day, and I slipped on the floor with my crutch as I got into the living room.

THANK GOD my family where there to hold me back up. That night as we were praying and singing to music, I cried to the song 'We pray for More' by Ntokozo Mbambo. THANKFUL to GOD for life.

My mum said her experience with our neighbour's wife was scary. She would be chanting and refusing to cooperate with the prayers, and it was like someone else was in her. Hours had gone past and she was still awake acting the same.

My mum could not fathom the reason behind her actions. As hours passed by, prayers increased. Galatians 6:9 reads, "And let us not grow weary of doing good, for in due season we will reap,

No, in all these things we are more than conquerors through him who loved us. For I am convinced that neither death nor life, neither angels nor demons, neither the present nor the future, nor any powers, neither height nor depth, nor anything else in all creation, will be able to separate us from the love of God that is in Christ Jesus our Lord (Romans 8: 37-39).

if we do not give up". We THANK GOD for the Spirit of wisdom and faith and giving us all strength. LORD YOU ARE AWESOME.

This comes to show how the effect of staying at home can overwhelm the mind. As an accountant, she worked from home, so maybe the pressure of working in the same place, in the same area with two noisy children at times impacted on her behaviour. In addition, her husband who worked at home, a professional in I.T. also had to adapt to this new temporary lifestyle.

It is important that you have someone to talk to about things you are feeling, or just to ask how did your day go? GOD is our friend. GOD is unsurpassed and Supreme over the whole Earth. In this situation they had each other but still went through that. GOD is ready to listen, help and add wisdom to our problems.

No, in all these things we are more than conquerors through him who loved us. For I am convinced that neither death nor life, neither angels nor demons, neither the present nor the future, nor any powers, neither height nor depth, nor anything else in all creation, will be able to separate us from the love of God that is in Christ Jesus our Lord (Romans 8: 37-39).

Day 55

It is May the sixteenth and today is a day full of Blessings. Today, TO THE GLORY OF ALMIGHT GOD because only GOD could have done it during these times, because my mum brought her car! Since October last year my mum had not had a car and for someone who loves to drive to most places she found this very hard. Taking the bus and constantly calling the taxi to go to places did not equal to the fun and love of driving your *own* car. My mum had saved up some money and brought her car. We really needed it in this time because taking the bus was not safe. In addition, we sometimes needed to give people food, and go to the food store for some essentials.

At times, we love to go for a ride to change our environment instead of always being at home.

I really THANK GOD because to buy a car during such a dangerous time, is not something I would have expected us to do. It still amazes me to this day; it puts a smile on my face because GOD is so merciful. It is not the typical car my mum would go for, but the mileage is good, and it works well.

Another Blessing we received was from a beautiful family who came on a Sunday to Bless us with loads of food. My favourite out of the thousands of foods given to us was the gigantic watermelon. It was like two of my heads and my head is kinda big.

No, in all these things we are more than conquerors through him who loved us. For I am convinced that neither death nor life, neither angels nor demons, neither the present nor the future, nor any powers, neither height nor depth, nor anything else in all creation, will be able to separate us from the love of God that is in Christ Jesus our Lord (Romans 8: 37-39).

They brought so much food that we still have some up till today, wow! By them Blessing us, it allowed us to branch the Blessings onto our neighbours, leaving them very happy to receive free food. GOD places such amazing people in our lives, and we will be forever grateful for this family.

THANK GOD ALMIGHTY!!

No, in all these things we are more than conquerors through him who loved us. For I am convinced that neither death nor life, neither angels nor demons, neither the present nor the future, nor any powers, neither height nor depth, nor anything else in all creation, will be able to separate us from the love of God that is in Christ Jesus our Lord (Romans 8: 37-39).

Day 64

Revenge
Against
Colored
In
Systematic
Methods
(RACISM)

Today… Today is May 25th 2020. It is the day that Mr George Floyd died due to police brutality. I didn't find out straight away. It was actually a few days after. In my head I though another black man dying, really! At this point I hadn't watched the video and honestly, I preferred not to see it. George Floyd was a 46-year-old man who died because of the insensitive behaviour of a group of 'policemen'. As said on Wikipedia, George Floyd, a 46-year-old black man, died in Minneapolis, Minnesota, after Derek Chauvin, a white police officer knelt on his neck for almost nine minutes while he was lying face down, handcuffed on the street. After being forced out his own car, aggressively handcuffed to the wall and knelt on his neck while being restricted by other policemen. It is sad. It is humiliating.

It is dehumanising. It is scary to see what the world is turning into. Slavery has been in effect for years. But this is modern slavery. Slavery to our feelings, slavery to our family and slavery to our lives but I believe with GOD all things are possible (Philippians 4:13).

No, in all these things we are more than conquerors through him who loved us. For I am convinced that neither death nor life, neither angels nor demons, neither the present nor the future, nor any powers, neither height nor depth, nor anything else in all creation, will be able to separate us from the love of God that is in Christ Jesus our Lord (Romans 8: 37-39).

According to Oxford Language Dictionary racism means prejudice, discrimination, or antagonism directed against someone of a different race based on the belief that one's own race is superior. And that is not okay. We are meant to be in unity and when they go low, we go high – Michelle Obama. When they continue to show hate, anger and cruelty, we have to show love. In fact, drown them with love because I believe their conscience will fight them within. The power of unity is very strong. We are strong and stronger together.

Black Lives Matter Protest in London, United Kingdom

No, in all these things we are more than conquerors through him who loved us. For I am convinced that neither death nor life, neither angels nor demons, neither the present nor the future, nor any powers, neither height nor depth, nor anything else in all creation, will be able to separate us from the love of God that is in Christ Jesus our Lord (Romans 8: 37-39).

Image above illustrated by Onamusi Timilehin Folagbade

No, in all these things we are more than conquerors through him who loved us. For I am convinced that neither death nor life, neither angels nor demons, neither the present nor the future, nor any powers, neither height nor depth, nor anything else in all creation, will be able to separate us from the love of God that is in Christ Jesus our Lord (Romans 8: 37-39).

Day 66

Today was children's day in Nigeria and it also happened to be my uncle's, who was quarantining with us, birthday as well. He has a twin, so we made sure he Zoomed into all the fun. At a little after twelve midnight, we said Happy Birthday and celebrated with a mini party accompanied by my uncle's twin brother social distancing from the phone. WhatsApp is an elite app, I can't lie.

Once quickly leaving behind the long line in Tesco we finished in time to participate in the WhatsApp call to the children. At 11:00am we had our first group of children. A minimum of 44 children joined on WhatsApp while we entertained them in our Praise & Worship dance, Mickey Mouse, Minnie Mouse and Michael Jackson.

We performed 'Power Flow' by Monique which is a powerful spiritual song and welcomed the Holy Spirit into our atmosphere. That song is lovely. All the children clapped and smiled as we performed for them. They loved it.

They were each promised a gift of their choice the next time we meet in Nigeria, BY THE GRACE OF GOD.

Then we called a family friend's two children in Nigeria and did a special performance for just the two of them, which we could tell that they loved because their smiles were from ear to ear.

As they saw the towering presents, they gasped in excitement at the possibilities that one of these gifts were for them. After choosing their gift they said thank you and we said goodbye.

No, in all these things we are more than conquerors through him who loved us. For I am convinced that neither death nor life, neither angels nor demons, neither the present nor the future, nor any powers, neither height nor depth, nor anything else in all creation, will be able to separate us from the love of God that is in Christ Jesus our Lord (Romans 8: 37-39).

Making children happy can make anyone happy. The song we played was called 'Heal the World' by Michael Jackson. It was very emotional because it was so relevant to our world today. The thought of how the world has grown in some ways good, but also in some ways bad, really bad, is devastating.

The news of knife crimes even on and off the news; children in school bullying other children; parents acting immature; false prophets making ridiculous allegations; women being taken advantage of; children being taken advantage of; boys being taken advantage of; men being taken advantage of; hate on the colour of peoples skin or on things that they

cannot change; being killed for one's belief or looks; the devil confusing the young and old minds on what they are and people killing each other for 'territory' as if we are animals. Hello here.... GOD owns the land, the Earth because He created it.

At 1:00pm we did a Zoom/Instagram party for all the children to see and be Blessed by it, in which all who joined will also receive gifts. The main focus is to make children happy and know that the love of GOD surrounds them.

There is no point 'following' GOD because your parents tell you to or because you go to Church with them every Sunday. You have to have your own relationship with God because the end time is near and 'GOD protects and BLESSES HIS people'.

Find someone you enjoy listening to preach. For example, Sarah Jake Roberts or Joyce Meyer and start of gradually. You can begin to pray and be led by The HOLY SPIRIT! A man called Bill Wiese gave an analogy along the lines of "well what if I am a good person my whole life, can I not go to HEAVEN?"

No, in all these things we are more than conquerors through him who loved us. For I am convinced that neither death nor life, neither angels nor demons, neither the present nor the future, nor any powers, neither height nor depth, nor anything else in all creation, will be able to separate us from the love of God that is in Christ Jesus our Lord (Romans 8: 37-39).

He then said "If you are a regular really nice person and you go to someone's house and say please can I stay here, their answer will be no. Why? Because we don't have a relationship with that person. So why should one enter HEAVEN if they do not have a relationship with God?"

I do think that is true because GOD longs and desires to have a relationship with us. No matter our flaws and mistakes. Yes, it is really true. GOD Loves us. You may have heard it so many times that JESUS is so forgiving, so why do you not believe it? Let us let God into our lives today and just accept GOD'S unconditional love towards us.

Genesis 1:27 reads, "So God created mankind in his own image, in the image of God he created them; male and female he created them." HALLELUJAH!

After entertaining our viewers for about two hours we had a two-hour break before the Zoom party at six o'clock. During those two hours that felt like two minutes, my sister and I cleared the kitchen from the mess we had made. We then made the top layer of the birthday cake, cleared the room upstairs, cooked BBQ chicken wings, BBQ drumsticks, the best prawns so far, corn on the cob and coleslaw. Wowz!

At six o clock we started the Zoom and people were Zooming in to celebrate the twins grand Birthday.

WE THANK GOD FOR LIFE AND ANOTHER YEAR FULL OF BLESSINGS AND UNDESERVING GRACE.

We sang a special requested song by my uncle which was 'Let Praises Rise' by Tyron Butler, and it was powerfully great. Then we hit some oldies songs, cut the delicious cake and had a Gospel artist sing to us on Zoom followed by potential Gospel artists, also referred to as family friends.

No, in all these things we are more than conquerors through him who loved us. For I am convinced that neither death nor life, neither angels nor demons, neither the present nor the future, nor any powers, neither height nor depth, nor anything else in all creation, will be able to separate us from the love of God that is in Christ Jesus our Lord (Romans 8: 37-39).

Lol. Even though the maximum limit on Zoom, without an upgrade is forty minutes, we exceeded that and hit the 'go again' button and went on for another forty minutes if not more. With our feet a bit sore from all the dancing we all sat down and ate while watching a Nollywood movie. Lately, we have been finding the modern ones rather intriguing, if I do say so myself.

Oh! How could I forget dessert? Sorry, I mean desserts. We also shared some food with family friends who live nearby. They came to pick it up contact free. It is weird saying that too, especially not being able to give them a hug when you see them. However, do not fret, we will soon BY GOD ALMIGHTY'S GRACE, AMENNN. Agh ☺. I Love GOD, man. GOD'S LOVE is so wonderful. Your love is so wide I cannot get around it, so low I cannot get under it, so high I cannot get over it. JESUS you give me wonderful LOVE. There is a song like that called 'Wonderful Love' by Ccioma. I especially love that she adapted it by adding her friends to it on Instagram. See, I am giving you guys tunes. No problem ohh.

I THANK GOD ALMIGHTY FOR SUCH A WONDERFUL DAY. WE COULD NOT HAVE DONE IT WITHOUT YOU GOD.

Visit the Relief Africa Charity Organization on www.reliefafrika.org.uk

No, in all these things we are more than conquerors through him who loved us. For I am convinced that neither death nor life, neither angels nor demons, neither the present nor the future, nor any powers, neither height nor depth, nor anything else in all creation, will be able to separate us from the love of God that is in Christ Jesus our Lord (Romans 8: 37-39).

Children's Day Virtual Celebration

During lockdown after we had the children's day celebration on Zoom, I decided to pretend that I was a news reporter and interviewed my mum about her charity organization Relief Africa.

No, in all these things we are more than conquerors through him who loved us. For I am convinced that neither death nor life, neither angels nor demons, neither the present nor the future, nor any powers, neither height nor depth, nor anything else in all creation, will be able to separate us from the love of God that is in Christ Jesus our Lord (Romans 8: 37-39).

No, in all these things we are more than conquerors through him who loved us. For I am convinced that neither death nor life, neither angels nor demons, neither the present nor the future, nor any powers, neither height nor depth, nor anything else in all creation, will be able to separate us from the love of God that is in Christ Jesus our Lord (Romans 8: 37-39).

BBC Feature with Mini-Misfit Lockdown Special

During the Lockdown I was involved in a series with a BBC programme hosted by Mini-Misfit called 'Lockdown Party'. After signing the consent forms and speaking to people in the team, I was given activities to do each week. The activities I would be doing were to cover ten weeks of the lockdown. It was really fun and exciting trying all the new activities, but sometimes I became frustrated because we had to do some things again so that it looked nice.

The first week we had to do an introduction type of video which showed us playing games with our family, doing things we wouldn't normally do as a family as a result of the pandemic. And walking our cute dog.

We decided that it was best to do a Tik Tok of 'Baby Girl Give me Something New' because in the beginning of lockdown it was trending.... a lot.

Other weeks included speaking of things that I wished to do after lockdown. I said missing my friends and giving to people in need. I cannot imagine how people who are alone are feeling, also the homeless and the elderly.

No, in all these things we are more than conquerors through him who loved us. For I am convinced that neither death nor life, neither angels nor demons, neither the present nor the future, nor any powers, neither height nor depth, nor anything else in all creation, will be able to separate us from the love of God that is in Christ Jesus our Lord (Romans 8: 37-39).

No, in all these things we are more than conquerors through him who loved us. For I am convinced that neither death nor life, neither angels nor demons, neither the present nor the future, nor any powers, neither height nor depth, nor anything else in all creation, will be able to separate us from the love of God that is in Christ Jesus our Lord (Romans 8: 37-39).

For many high school students, going to prom is a rite of passage and a highlight of the academic year. It's a time they get to ignore schoolwork, dress up and have fun with their friends (BBC, 2020).

In another week I did a Prom video. As I am part of the class of 2020, we did not get to have our leaver's assembly, our prom or anything like that. So, BBC gave some of us the chance to transform from a scruffy look to our prom dress look.

Warning: The picture of my prom dress is not my actual one. My actual one would be a cutie plus quarantine belly trying to take over.

No, in all these things we are more than conquerors through him who loved us. For I am convinced that neither death nor life, neither angels nor demons, neither the present nor the future, nor any powers, neither height nor depth, nor anything else in all creation, will be able to separate us from the love of God that is in Christ Jesus our Lord (Romans 8: 37-39).

Each week consisted of fun things to do. It involved dancing, doing popular challenges, saying something about lockdown, dressing up and playing games. This really helped to keep me busy and active because each task was different and surprising. Some were even competitive.

One of my favourite speeches that I shared on BBC was my Black Lives Matter speech, 'Black Lives Matter'.

Black Lives Matter is not just a collection of nouns and words. It is not just a trending hashtag or a one-day post, but a verb. A verb, we are taught, is a doing word, so we will do it. We will make Black Lives Matter. I urge you first of all, to pray for all people. Ask GOD to help them intercede on their behalf and give thanks for them. "Pray this way for kings and those who are in authority so that we can live peaceful and quiet lives marked by godliness and dignity. This is good and pleases GOD" (1 Timothy 2:13). I can breathe and the only way to speak up for what is right is through my breath so justice can/will prevail. The Sprit of GOD has made me, and the breath of the Almighty gives me life.

Participating in the BBC series 'Lockdown Party' was a memorable experience and it is going to be part of History. I think of us, when we overcome this Covid-19, talking to our children and grandchildren about this. Or that it could possibly be in history books in the future.

The protests continues...

No, in all these things we are more than conquerors through him who loved us. For I am convinced that neither death nor life, neither angels nor demons, neither the present nor the future, nor any powers, neither height nor depth, nor anything else in all creation, will be able to separate us from the love of God that is in Christ Jesus our Lord (Romans 8: 37-39).

Self-Evaluation

I must say this quarantine has taught me a lot, most of all to be thankful. Not just thankful for GOD adding another year to my life, or thankful for money or food, or thankful for going shopping, or just being thankful for waking up that morning. Me being thankful has more value and meaning to it now. THANK YOU, LORD for all the things it takes to get up. THANK YOU for giving me the strength to wake up and to get out of bed; the ability to move my limbs; to open my eyes and see things around me; to desire to do more things; to help GOD's KINGDOM and people and to better myself. I try to live everyday as it was my last because it helps remind us that we don't know when our time is up on Earth, so how can you make a change? Death can be a sad thing, a time when all emotions are high but if you think of all you can do to help people in the entire world, then it changes your mindset about death. It widens your mindset on how to live life. Quarantine has taught me to plan things strategically, even though I am not there yet, I am still learning. One of the few things we find hard to do is to be happy with where we are in life. Be happy in every part of it because GOD has brought us this far. Why, oh why, oh why, will GOD leave you now?

Being happy where you are does not mean you have lost the motivation to keep on progressing. We should still aim to move from Glory to Glory and impact more people.

Because of where I am now does not mean I will be in the same place forever.

Because I am contempt does not mean I will not show my greatness or perseverance even more.

No, in all these things we are more than conquerors through him who loved us. For I am convinced that neither death nor life, neither angels nor demons, neither the present nor the future, nor any powers, neither height nor depth, nor anything else in all creation, will be able to separate us from the love of God that is in Christ Jesus our Lord (Romans 8: 37-39).

Because I am satisfied with where I am now does not mean I will reduce my Praise and Glory to GOD. Hallelujah!

The only way is up. GLORY HALLELUJAH! After listening to Stephanie Ike over the period of two evenings, it made me realise that I have surrendered my special thing of work that

gives me fire from within and makes me think far beyond of all the things that I will do, BY THE GRACE OF ALMIGHTY GOD.

My thing that sees me flourishing from Glory to Glory; reaching for far beyond the sky and maximising my abilities and skills to do things that no one else can do but me, because we are all different. At times we need to think out of the box and not chase after the occupation of someone else. No one is the same, even identical twins have a different DNA. And if it happens to be that you have the same desires or aims as someone else, what makes your way unique, apart from being you?

Sometimes we tend to give up things when we do not see anything working or we do not see profit from it. When we a make a sacrifice to GOD, GOD knows we are serious. It does not have to be money. It can be time, clothes for someone who needs it more or anything given up (something valued) for the sake of other's considerations.

We need to spend time in GOD'S Presence in order to get a revelation or vision of what GOD wants us to do. This goes for me too. Being successful does not mean making stacks of money and being known worldwide. There may have been that one specific person that needed your service which alternated their life forever.

No, in all these things we are more than conquerors through him who loved us. For I am convinced that neither death nor life, neither angels nor demons, neither the present nor the future, nor any powers, neither height nor depth, nor anything else in all creation, will be able to separate us from the love of God that is in Christ Jesus our Lord (Romans 8: 37-39).

Waiting on GOD can seem *long* and hard at times, but it is for a reason. Stephanie Ike said in her preaching on 'Posture of Prayer' that the same age of a girl in the BIBLE who had died (twelve years) was the same age as the woman who had the issue of blood. The same year the young girl was born was the same year the lady had an issue of blood. God had been on the earth before this and he could have healed the lady before that, but everything happens for a reason. The year you start to develop that burning desire could be the birth of someone's breakthrough.

Let me say it again for clarity purposes, the year you decide to develop that burning desire that has been within you. The one that made you thinks far and beyond, for some for so long, is the year someone's breakthrough is being birthed. Let us be patient. Also, trying to listen to GOD is important. The BIBLE says in Psalms 37:23-25, "The steps of a good man are ordered by the LORD: and he delights in his way". GOD is the ULTIMATE plan maker, Rule maker and Sustainer over our life. So, listening to GOD with nothing distracting us will help us to have access to GOD'S voice.

Another thing I have come to a near understanding of, is being obedient. At times we feel like why do we need to do this or that, but even being obedient to the small things matters.

I feel that during this quarantine GOD told me to be obedient, hopefully I am trying my best. What do you feel you are being called to do after this lockdown or even during this lockdown?

No, in all these things we are more than conquerors through him who loved us. For I am convinced that neither death nor life, neither angels nor demons, neither the present nor the future, nor any powers, neither height nor depth, nor anything else in all creation, will be able to separate us from the love of God that is in Christ Jesus our Lord (Romans 8: 37-39).

Image illustrated by Chinyere Anosike

No, in all these things we are more than conquerors through him who loved us. For I am convinced that neither death nor life, neither angels nor demons, neither the present nor the future, nor any powers, neither height nor depth, nor anything else in all creation, will be able to separate us from the love of God that is in Christ Jesus our Lord (Romans 8: 37-39).

Day 71

It is now June the 1st. Six days after the devastating and unnecessary death of Mr George Floyd and the world is still in shock. Day after day the news spread, newspapers are picking it up, magazines, Instagram pages, Twitter, Snapchat, CNN News, BBC News and so many more. I cannot even begin to imagen how his family are feeling, especially his daughter. As young as she is, I do not think she has fully comprehended the meaning of this all. That video of her father being murdered is online which I am sure she will see when she is older. LORD, I Pray for Peace that surpasses all understanding to dwell in their family and the world. I Pray this shall be a time for the whole world to draw closer to you and experience your Glorious Presence. By this time, I had watched the horrific video and my heart hurt for him. Even though someone had checked his pulse, that man continued to leave his knee on George Floyd's neck.

That is no way to treat a human being, anyone. I believe there was intent to harm Mr Floyd and most likely to kill him, because of the fact that he did not think zero seconds was enough, so he went on for nine minutes! And the fact that his knee was placed on his neck, which is the only way Mr Floyd could breathe properly. The help of the former policemen also played a big part in this murder, because there was no way for Mr Floyd to break out of that bondage they put him in. He is now a heroic figure. Thank you.

Unfortunately, Mr Floyd was in bondage by the police officers, it was like they were possessed by negativity because the other 'police officer' did not even budge or react respectfully to the situation. Fortunately, for us, we do not have to stay in that bondage through the help of GOD

No, in all these things we are more than conquerors through him who loved us. For I am convinced that neither death nor life, neither angels nor demons, neither the present nor the future, nor any powers, neither height nor depth, nor anything else in all creation, will be able to separate us from the love of God that is in Christ Jesus our Lord (Romans 8: 37-39).

because we are more than conquers. Just as it says in Romans 8:37, 37, "Yet in all these things we are more than conquerors and gain an overwhelming victory through Him who loved us [so much that He died for us]". We are called to conquer. GOD has given us all the resources we need and the ones we did not even know we had.

"He who overcomes [the world through believing that Jesus is the Son of God], I will grant to him [the privilege] to sit beside Me on My throne, as I also overcame and sat down beside My Father on His throne" (Revelation 3:21).

The day the protests began.

No, in all these things we are more than conquerors through him who loved us. For I am convinced that neither death nor life, neither angels nor demons, neither the present nor the future, nor any powers, neither height nor depth, nor anything else in all creation, will be able to separate us from the love of God that is in Christ Jesus our Lord (Romans 8: 37-39).

Day 72

It is day 2 of the protests and there have been fires in buildings, banners held during the marches, people robbing stores, peaceful marches, and long walks along the roads, artwork and people expressing their feelings in many ways. Thousands of people gathered to join in the protest, mixed race, blacks, whites, Asians and many more ethnic backgrounds. It was truly amazing to see so many people join in unity to express their feelings of unfairness in the 'justice system'. As Pastor Matthew Ashimolowo said, "After the protest how do you plan to make a change?

No, in all these things we are more than conquerors through him who loved us. For I am convinced that neither death nor life, neither angels nor demons, neither the present nor the future, nor any powers, neither height nor depth, nor anything else in all creation, will be able to separate us from the love of God that is in Christ Jesus our Lord (Romans 8: 37-39).

Day 73

It is day 3 of the protest and the love has now travelled all around the World. Many more are protesting. The attendances are increasing, and the impact is increasing. Young and old went out pleading for justice. On one young boy's banner it read, 'Am I next?' That was painful and it really hurt to see that. He was probably no younger than seven. He was already thinking negative thoughts about his future instead of dreaming to be whatever he wanted to be, what GOD wants him to be.

No, in all these things we are more than conquerors through him who loved us. For I am convinced that neither death nor life, neither angels nor demons, neither the present nor the future, nor any powers, neither height nor depth, nor anything else in all creation, will be able to separate us from the love of God that is in Christ Jesus our Lord (Romans 8: 37-39).

Day 75

It is about day 5 of the protest and in London thousands of people gathered in unity to protest for Justice. Actresses, actors, influencers, TV Personalities and many more, just as important people protested for what they believe in. It was actually surprising to see such a vast majority of white people attending. I strongly believe that made a bold statement. Not everyone has the same intentions. Whether some were there for social media 'performance' or insincere reasons, they added to the crowd which showed the government the drastic need for change.

I just do not know why there cannot be a law to treat humans, especially black people, *as* humans! My mother and uncle watched the evening news about the protests. Glaring into the television, they said there has not been a movement as big as this before, all around the world. They suggested Mr Rodney King or Martin Luther King Jr, but still they said this one was different. It wasn't quite the same.

No, in all these things we are more than conquerors through him who loved us. For I am convinced that neither death nor life, neither angels nor demons, neither the present nor the future, nor any powers, neither height nor depth, nor anything else in all creation, will be able to separate us from the love of God that is in Christ Jesus our Lord (Romans 8: 37-39).

Day 80

Seven days into the protest and it was still marching on as strong as the first day. The energy was booming. I even think that it was stronger as the days grew because more people were involved and supporting one another. Seeing more people take part even gave people like me who could not attend the protests to share our pain and passion on social media. During the ongoing protests there were certain social media trends such as 'Black Out Tuesday'.

But no, instead of 'Black Out Tuesday', as my Aunty Elizabeth said we should spread light. We are the light. "I saw that wisdom is better than folly, just as light is better than darkness, so we overcome darkness" (Ecclesiastes 2:13).

Those who were chanting 'can't breathe, no, I *can* breathe because Job 33:4 says, "The Spirit of God has made me, and the breath of the Almighty gives me life." If we had no breath, we would not be able to speak for justice and make a change in the world.

"Let everything that has breath praise the Lord! Praise the Lord" (Psalm 150:6).

No, in all these things we are more than conquerors through him who loved us. For I am convinced that neither death nor life, neither angels nor demons, neither the present nor the future, nor any powers, neither height nor depth, nor anything else in all creation, will be able to separate us from the love of God that is in Christ Jesus our Lord (Romans 8: 37-39).

Day 87

Fifteen long days in and the protests were still transpiring, all the way to Senegal, South Africa, Paris, Ghana and across the globe. It was uplifting to see the unity across the World.

However, some people thought otherwise. A group of far-right believers conspired to fight against the Black Lives Matter Movement and cause a chaotic scene that included harming the police and destroying areas. As said on Wikipedia, 'Far-right politics also referred to as the extreme right or right-wing extremism, are politics further on the right of the left–right spectrum than the standard political right, particularly in terms of extreme nationalism, nativist ideologies and authoritarian tendencies.' I believe they truly are far from right, but hey, we all need GOD'S mercy.

Despite the negative views against Black Lives Matter, when an injured far-right needed aid a Black Lives Matter protestor carried him and gave him aid. That speaks a lot. Hopefully, the far–right believer will consider and change his views.

No, in all these things we are more than conquerors through him who loved us. For I am convinced that neither death nor life, neither angels nor demons, neither the present nor the future, nor any powers, neither height nor depth, nor anything else in all creation, will be able to separate us from the love of God that is in Christ Jesus our Lord (Romans 8: 37-39).

Day 88

Rayshard Brooks. Sigh. Rayshard brook was a twenty-seven-year old man who was shot by the Atlanta police department on the 12th of June 2020. Another victim caught in the net of police brutality. The wickedness in high places. He admitted to drinking which probably caused him to sleep in the line for food at Wendy's but shooting him especially after the death of George Floyd felt like wickedness in high places to me. It felt like abuse of authority. It felt like misuse of undeserving power. It felt like racism. This man was only able to live to see twenty-seven years and missed the continuous celebration of his child's birthday, leaving behind his children. That is devastating. The more we dislike things the more we have to do. Change will not happen without you. As Pastor Matthew Ashemolowo said, "There are many black people working in the same field but what about the field that 'they' would not expect us to work in?" Black people have to change the spaces of work where white people dominate. When someone asks us, what do we work as we want to shock them with our confident responses. Where we live, how we live or the limitations that has been said to us, does not determine our future.

"For I know the plans I have for you," declares the Lord, "plans to prosper you and not to harm you, plans to give you hope and a future" (Jeremiah 29:11 (NIV) New International Version). Only GOD and us. What are changing with these protests?

No, in all these things we are more than conquerors through him who loved us. For I am convinced that neither death nor life, neither angels nor demons, neither the present nor the future, nor any powers, neither height nor depth, nor anything else in all creation, will be able to separate us from the love of God that is in Christ Jesus our Lord (Romans 8: 37-39).

Day 90

In Memory of My Friend

That morning I woke up to the sound of a scream bellowing from downstairs. Followed by a puzzled but sorrowful voice, talking in despair also coming from downstairs. I knelt down to pray, as I usually do and strolled downstairs as I wiped the morning look of my face. I saw my mum and sister sitting on the couch pinned to their phone in disbelief of something. From upstairs I could vaguely here what was said, but I choose not to believe it, I decided to summarise it as a misunderstanding.

Now, let's go back a few months. In February of 2020, my sisters travelled to Tallahassee, Florida for the funeral of my late grandad's brother. During their stay there they met a beautiful bubbly girl called Toyin. Toyin was around the same age as my third sister but she was older by a few months. My two older sisters enjoyed her company and spent some of their time in Tallahassee going to Walmart with Toyin and others or to family gatherings.

They conversed on personal feelings, shared clothing, and uplifted each other. Toyin stayed at our auntie's house which is where my sisters were staying too for the duration of their trip. They all developed a bond and Toyin's welcoming heart made them feel as if she was family.

Returning from their trip, they both stayed in contact with Toyin and showed their love for her.

The conversation about coming to London in October for my sister's event had surfaced, among other topics.

No, in all these things we are more than conquerors through him who loved us. For I am convinced that neither death nor life, neither angels nor demons, neither the present nor the future, nor any powers, neither height nor depth, nor anything else in all creation, will be able to separate us from the love of God that is in Christ Jesus our Lord (Romans 8: 37-39).

Toyin called my mother and I on our birthdays and I was so excited to meet her in the future. At the age of nineteen she acted like a mature lady. As an overcomer of many hardships in her life, that probably gave her courage to be stronger. Toyin believed in the Word of GOD and as her friend said, "She was growing in her relationship with GOD".

On June 6th it was brought to our attention through social media that after attending or while protesting she had been missing. The Tallahassee police department put up a missing person's poster with her picture and description below in the hope of finding her. Our cousin in American and some other people conducted a search party in order to find her.

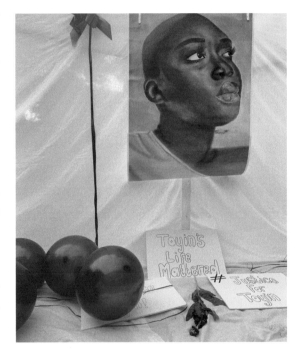

On Saturday June 13th, she was found dead.

As written by Wikipedia, Oluwatoyin Ruth "Toyin" Salau was a Black Lives Matter activist who disappeared on Saturday June 6, 2020, shortly after tweeting about being sexually assaulted.

Salau was found dead in Tallahassee, Florida on Saturday June 13, 2020, and her death was confirmed on Monday June 15, 2020.

On June 15th we heard the news. My sister cried out in disbelief, that someone who she had spoken to days before could be gone, just like that. At that instant I felt numb. Numb to the

No, in all these things we are more than conquerors through him who loved us. For I am convinced that neither death nor life, neither angels nor demons, neither the present nor the future, nor any powers, neither height nor depth, nor anything else in all creation, will be able to separate us from the love of God that is in Christ Jesus our Lord (Romans 8: 37-39).

sound around me. Numb to the pain. Numb to how I though she must have felt in those last few seconds she had to breathe.

It may be hard to believe but, after wondering if it was true, all I could do was just Worship and give Praise to GOD, not because she was dead but because what else could I do? I don't want to say something I could regret or sin.

Prior to this heart-wrenching news, I happened to watch a preacher speak of a story of a man and woman who were about to sign their marriage certificate. As the woman was about to sign her marriage certificate her husband dropped to the ground and died. They prayed and asked GOD to help him and let him wake up, let him live again but nothing happened.

Then someone remembered a BIBLE Scripture about giving thanks and Praise to GOD, so they did. A short while after giving thanks to GOD our LORD, the man came back to life again and asked, "Why am I on the floor?" With that story at the back of my mind, I thought that it might work in this circumstance. In Ecclesiastes 3: 1-2 it says, "There is a time for everything, and a season for every activity under the heavens: a time to be born and a time to die." GOD is in control.

I could not believe it. In fact, I didn't want to believe it. She was only nineteen and had so much to do. At the age of nineteen she had been through so much and learned so much, that I was convinced anything she wanted to pursue in the future was achievable. She was a woman of courage.

I do believe that we should all check on our friends, family, people we have lost contact with and even those who we may have had an argument with.

No, in all these things we are more than conquerors through him who loved us. For I am convinced that neither death nor life, neither angels nor demons, neither the present nor the future, nor any powers, neither height nor depth, nor anything else in all creation, will be able to separate us from the love of God that is in Christ Jesus our Lord (Romans 8: 37-39).

On the outside they may look fine, but what is going on the inside? Be an advocate of change. This does not mean every friend or people we know are down, but we all have some sad days and we need one another to help us get back up stronger.

No, in all these things we are more than conquerors through him who loved us. For I am convinced that neither death nor life, neither angels nor demons, neither the present nor the future, nor any powers, neither height nor depth, nor anything else in all creation, will be able to separate us from the love of God that is in Christ Jesus our Lord (Romans 8: 37-39).

Day 97

My Friend's Memorial Service

We had a memorial service for her here in London while people and family joined on Zoom, Instagram and Facebook. I knew that it was going to be a hard day but, on that day, it felt even harder. Each of us spoke, accompanied by other people who wished to speak. For some they couldn't because the wound was too fresh. I understand. Even some of her friends from America spoke. We prayed, ministered in dance, and sang some Worship songs that was befitting to the mood. While my sisters were in America, they recalled her confessing her love for African music. Although it was not a Christian song, we danced to a song she liked called 'Beginning' by Joeboy. "I'm beginning, beginning to fall in LOVE". We love you Toyin, and I pray GOD open His arms and welcome you to your new mansion in HEAVEN. We made an altar call, which is giving your life to CHRIST.

Image above illustrated by Onamusi Timilehin Folagbade

No, in all these things we are more than conquerors through him who loved us. For I am convinced that neither death nor life, neither angels nor demons, neither the present nor the future, nor any powers, neither height nor depth, nor anything else in all creation, will be able to separate us from the love of God that is in Christ Jesus our Lord (Romans 8: 37-39).

If you simply say, "LORD JESUS come into my life. I need you today and always as my LORD and personal Saviour. I cannot live a fulfilled life without YOU, LORD so please stay with me. I believe JESUS died for my sins and resurrected three days later. I want to do YOUR will and YOUR will alone. I want to obey YOU. Thank you, LORD, for saving me."

Congratulations! Get ready for a BLESSED life.

We released twenty balloons, and an extra one for extra blessings. And a short while after, we sang along with this song, 'Something Inside so Strong' by Labi Siffre. Releasing the balloons is not us forgetting her, instead it is releasing the pain.

Toyin was a strong and brave girl, a strong woman. She gave herself no limitations. I really wish I had met her, but I know everything is for a reason. I am glad my sisters met her. She impacted our lives and people all around the world. She impacted the protestors lives, famous people, popular magazines such as Essence, Cosmopolitan and, BET (Black Entertainment Television) and hopefully now you. Her voice was heard, and we will try our best to continue to make it heard.

No, in all these things we are more than conquerors through him who loved us. For I am convinced that neither death nor life, neither angels nor demons, neither the present nor the future, nor any powers, neither height nor depth, nor anything else in all creation, will be able to separate us from the love of God that is in Christ Jesus our Lord (Romans 8: 37-39).

All About Angel

As this book is coming to a close, it would only be right to acknowledge a lovely girl in our family's life, Angel.

Angel. Where do I start with Angel? She truly is an Angel. This beautiful girl is always there by the door when I am about to open the door. Occasionally, she hastily gets the mail before anyone else so that she can give it to you first as if it is a competition. Having her during Lockdown especially, and even before Lockdown has been a true Blessing. While we pray, she lays with us, gracing us with her peaceful presence. She is the best dog ever! When you're upset or angry, she can just tell. Slowly licking your feet to make you feel better or playfully jumping on you with her front two paws clenching onto your shoulder so that she is high enough to lick your face. Having Angel for nearly six years has been costly and fun. She fits in our family so well. She completes part of the puzzle. I remember when she was no more than three months old and I was so scared of her. I didn't even know how scared of dogs I was until she actually entered the house after a three hours long drive. Funny enough, my mum was going to turn back because she was tired halfway along the journey to somewhere, she did not know and something that might not be true. She was probably thinking all of this for a dog! Eventually, the seller agreed to meet halfway so that it works best for both of them. I remember that day, anxious to what she would look like and how she would act. I cannot imagine these past years without her. If she could speak, she would probably tell me off when I get annoyed because she is in the way, but overall, it is all love. Love conquers all.

No, in all these things we are more than conquerors through him who loved us. For I am convinced that neither death nor life, neither angels nor demons, neither the present nor the future, nor any powers, neither height nor depth, nor anything else in all creation, will be able to separate us from the love of God that is in Christ Jesus our Lord (Romans 8: 37-39).

Angel was comforting during Lockdown and made each day less dreadful because of her new shenanigans. If she was not barking at birds or chasing the once in a while foxes that appeared in the garden, then she would have sneaked herself into the neighbour's garden through her secret tunnel. Well, thanks Angel for being so cute and getting cuter each month, day, second.

I love you lots.

Family dog "Angel"

No, in all these things we are more than conquerors through him who loved us. For I am convinced that neither death nor life, neither angels nor demons, neither the present nor the future, nor any powers, neither height nor depth, nor anything else in all creation, will be able to separate us from the love of God that is in Christ Jesus our Lord (Romans 8: 37-39).

Words of Encouragement

Do not start something you are not willing to complete! As I was writing, I was about to just write the title and call it a day. In certain circumstances we have to push our self to get the best out of us and sew the best seed we can. We need to be ready for the harvest.

Never give up! No matter how hard it seems. I really feel that is for someone. GOD is nothing but merciful and GOD is faithful until the end. I LOVE GOD. Do not go for something because you think you need it to live. NO, you only need it to survive. Why not live? Live the life GOD has for you. The BIBLE says…

It is good to be optimistic. The sudden virus hit us all with a surprise and for some people they lost their lives, or a loved one has lost their life, or they know someone who knows someone who has. No matter what it is still a life.

Whenever I think of someone who has died I think of them themselves that they have lost their life; then their immediate family; then the outer family; then family friends and friends; the work colleagues; and the friends who lost contact even to the person who they may not have known but spoke to the day before. Look at all those people impacted by that life. Nevertheless, the thousands of people who have lost their lives to the virus.

No, in all these things we are more than conquerors through him who loved us. For I am convinced that neither death nor life, neither angels nor demons, neither the present nor the future, nor any powers, neither height nor depth, nor anything else in all creation, will be able to separate us from the love of God that is in Christ Jesus our Lord (Romans 8: 37-39).

To this date, June 1st 12:33 am, 371K+5,017 have died due to the coronavirus worldwide. Imagine all those family members, friends, and I am sure some people know some of the same people who have died, making them carry another burden.

"Be strong and courageous. Do not be afraid or terrified because of them, for the LORD your God goes with you; he will never leave you or forsake you" (Deuteronomy 31:6). There are more verses in the BIBLE where GOD ALMIGHTY reassures us of our safety and wellbeing so we have to put our faith in GOD even though it may seem tough. I believe the LORD is coming soon and we should prepare by trying to live a righteous life.

We should not be scared because where we are going is far better, and we are promised eternity with our Father in Heaven. "Behold, I am coming soon, bringing my recompense with me, to repay everyone for what he has done. I am the Alpha and the Omega, the first and the last, the beginning and the end" (Revelation 22: 12-13).

"In my Father's house are many mansions: if it were not so, I would have told you. I go to prepare a place for you" (John 14:2).

"But make sure that you don't get so absorbed and exhausted in taking care of all your day-by-day obligations that you lose track of the time and doze off, oblivious to God. The night is about over, dawn is about to break. Be up and awake to what God is doing! God is putting the finishing touches on the salvation work he began when we first believed. We can't afford to waste a minute, must not squander these precious daylight hours in frivolity and indulgence, in sleeping around and dissipation, in bickering and grabbing everything in sight. Get out of bed and get dressed! Don't loiter and linger, waiting until the very last minute. Dress yourselves in Christ and be up and about! (Romans 13:11-14 (MSG) The Message).

No, in all these things we are more than conquerors through him who loved us. For I am convinced that neither death nor life, neither angels nor demons, neither the present nor the future, nor any powers, neither height nor depth, nor anything else in all creation, will be able to separate us from the love of God that is in Christ Jesus our Lord (Romans 8: 37-39).

I feel as if these scriptures all speak for themselves. Let us all try to be righteous and live right with GOD. If we have any worries or issues, we can talk to GOD because HE will always listen, ultimate friend.

A preacher once said that sometimes we should go for something and if it is right or wrong for us, our conscious will let us know. We can feel a gap within our life or anxieties whether we are doing something right or not, but how do we overcome that? With the help of GOD, it is made easier to make choices and feel at peace.

"The steps of a [good and righteous] man are directed and established by the Lord, And He delights in his way [and blesses his path]" (Psalm 37: 23). The word man is another word for people. None of us are perfect and we will sin many times but accepting GOD into our life opens the door to forgiveness and happiness in our life.

If you are trying to start your journey with CHRIST JESUS, here are a few tips I think can help:

1. Giving your life to GOD, saying the prayer and fully meaning it.

2. Being ready for all that GOD has in store for you.

3. Having the Bible App! So important.

4. Praying. It can be 15 minutes in the morning then 20 at night.

5. Choosing Bible plans. Start off with one at a time then you can progress to more, trust me.

6. Reading the Bible every day from the verse of the day to whatever you feel led to read.

No, in all these things we are more than conquerors through him who loved us. For I am convinced that neither death nor life, neither angels nor demons, neither the present nor the future, nor any powers, neither height nor depth, nor anything else in all creation, will be able to separate us from the love of God that is in Christ Jesus our Lord (Romans 8: 37-39).

7. Listening and learning from preachers. Make sure the preacher you watch teaches about GOD'S law, the Bible will help you know about false prophets and as you spiritually grow, your conscience will help you.

8. Having an appropriate elder to talk about GOD with.

9. Having a Church that you can attend. It helps to be in fellowship with others.

10. Trusting GOD, no matter what and having faith.

No, in all these things we are more than conquerors through him who loved us. For I am convinced that neither death nor life, neither angels nor demons, neither the present nor the future, nor any powers, neither height nor depth, nor anything else in all creation, will be able to separate us from the love of God that is in Christ Jesus our Lord (Romans 8: 37-39).

Ministries Outreach

Contact Me via
emmanuellainfo@gmail.com
@theellls – Youtube, Twitter, Facebook & Instagram

No, in all these things we are more than conquerors through him who loved us. For I am convinced that neither death nor life, neither angels nor demons, neither the present nor the future, nor any powers, neither height nor depth, nor anything else in all creation, will be able to separate us from the love of God that is in Christ Jesus our Lord (Romans 8: 37-39).

Relief Africa Charity
www.reliefafrika.org.uk

Praise & Worship dance ministers
www.thelevitesworship.com

Mr & Miss Teen Nigeria UK https://mmtnuk.com/

ReachOut2All CIC Youth Organization
www.reachout2all.co.uk

Chrissy's Cuisine
Instagram- @c__cuisine

Concerning the publication, there are two artists known as Onamusi Timilehin Folagbade & Chinyere Anosike involved in the project. This was a chance to display their talents and also a portrayal of unwasted gifts during the Covid-19 pandemic.

These are youths we supported and paid during this critical era. We ask you also to support them in their skills as we encourage other youths to thrive in their talents.

Please contact them via remiadejokun@yahoo.co.uk.

God bless you.

No, in all these things we are more than conquerors through him who loved us. For I am convinced that neither death nor life, neither angels nor demons, neither the present nor the future, nor any powers, neither height nor depth, nor anything else in all creation, will be able to separate us from the love of God that is in Christ Jesus our Lord (Romans 8: 37-39).

Gallery of my lockdown during THE PANDEMIC

No, in all these things we are more than conquerors through him who loved us. For I am convinced that neither death nor life, neither angels nor demons, neither the present nor the future, nor any powers, neither height nor depth, nor anything else in all creation, will be able to separate us from the love of God that is in Christ Jesus our Lord (Romans 8: 37-39).

No, in all these things we are more than conquerors through him who loved us. For I am convinced that neither death nor life, neither angels nor demons, neither the present nor the future, nor any powers, neither height nor depth, nor anything else in all creation, will be able to separate us from the love of God that is in Christ Jesus our Lord (Romans 8: 37-39).

A BIRTHDAY
CAKE FOR A
FAMILY FRIEND

No, in all these things we are more than conquerors through him who loved us. For I am convinced that neither death nor life, neither angels nor demons, neither the present nor the future, nor any powers, neither height nor depth, nor anything else in all creation, will be able to separate us from the love of God that is in Christ Jesus our Lord (Romans 8: 37-39).

ATTEMPTING TO DO NAILS, YIKES

No, in all these things we are more than conquerors through him who loved us. For I am convinced that neither death nor life, neither angels nor demons, neither the present nor the future, nor any powers, neither height nor depth, nor anything else in all creation, will be able to separate us from the love of God that is in Christ Jesus our Lord (Romans 8: 37-39).

Remi & her Girls as Elvis and the Supremes

No, in all these things we are more than conquerors through him who loved us. For I am convinced that neither death nor life, neither angels nor demons, neither the present nor the future, nor any powers, neither height nor depth, nor anything else in all creation, will be able to separate us from the love of God that is in Christ Jesus our Lord (Romans 8: 37-39).

TO BE CONTINUED......

No, in all these things we are more than conquerors through him who loved us. For I am convinced that neither death nor life, neither angels nor demons, neither the present nor the future, nor any powers, neither height nor depth, nor anything else in all creation, will be able to separate us from the love of God that is in Christ Jesus our Lord (Romans 8: 37-39).

References

Metro News
https://metro.co.uk/2020/04/19/first-case-coronavirus-uk-covid-19-diagnosis-12578061/
World health COVID-19 report 2020. Coronavirus. Europe, World Health Organization, 2020.
https://www.who.int/health-topics/coronavirus#tab=tab_1

No, in all these things we are more than conquerors through him who loved us. For I am convinced that neither death nor life, neither angels nor demons, neither the present nor the future, nor any powers, neither height nor depth, nor anything else in all creation, will be able to separate us from the love of God that is in Christ Jesus our Lord (Romans 8: 37-39).

Who Am I

Emmanuella Alausa is a sixteen years old Author who is currently getting ready for her A Levels. She has been nominated for The British Citizen Youth Award, True Little Hero Award, celebrating Young People Award, recognised by MP Steve Reed House of Commons and received an Award for 'Future Young Star' by AAA4Success.

She is the fourth child out of three older siblings who are also girls including a cute dog too. Ever since she was a young girl she has always been friendly and bubbly, ready to have a conversation with you and make her opinions know. As a young girl Emmanuella has thousands of ambitions that she is dedicated to achieve for example starting an Organisation to help children in need, securing a degree and spreading the Love of GOD. When often asked the question "What do you want to be when you're older", she replies with a list of possibilities, giving herself no limitations.

Her first book 'My Prayer Shawl', which she wrote at the age of thirteen, is a prayer book for children between the ages of four to sixteen. She has a great fondness for children, always wanting to be around them. Emmanuella wrote this book with the aim to allow children to have a relationship with GOD and to be able to have a strong foundation, giving them the only option, levelling up. She loves to pray also know as the prayer warrior.

Around the age of thirteen Emmanuella attended a leading Performing Arts and Technology School know as Brit School where she would practice Street Dance, she has an inspiration of being an Actress and recently obtained a role in a short film, she is a progressing motivational speaker and an ambassador to ReachOut2All. She attempts to cook but sometimes her creativity overpowers the flavour. Predominantly helping others is what she deeply wants to achieve. Emmanuella says "What is the point of living if you don't help someone else?".

No, in all these things we are more than conquerors through him who loved us. For I am convinced that neither death nor life, neither angels nor demons, neither the present nor the future, nor any powers, neither height nor depth, nor anything else in all creation, will be able to separate us from the love of God that is in Christ Jesus our Lord (Romans 8: 37-39).

Printed in the United States
By Bookmasters